JAMAKE HIGHWATER

Songs for the Seasons

ILLUSTRATIONS BY SANDRA SPEIDEL

LOTHROP, LEE & SHEPARD BOOKS   NEW YORK

The illustrations in this book were done in chalk pastels on watercolor paper. The display type was set in Greyton Script. The text was set in Cochin Bold. Printed and bound by Tien Wah Press. Production supervision by Bonnie King. Designed by Robin Ballard.

First Edition   1 2 3 4 5 6 7 8 9 10
Library of Congress Cataloging in Publication Data. Highwater, Jamake. Songs for the seasons / Jamake Highwater; illustrated by Sandra Speidel.
p.   cm.   Summary: Each season's song describes the changes that occur in nature as the year moves from summer through fall and winter to spring.
ISBN 0-688-10658-7. — ISBN 0-688-10659-5 (lib.bdg.) 1. Seasons—Poetry. 2. Children's poetry, American. I. Speidel, Sandra, ill. II. Title.
PS3558.I373S66 1994 811'. 54—dc20 93-8094 CIP AC

FOR ROBERTA AND PETER MARKMAN
Once we have scorched our brains,
we can plunge to Hell or Heaven,
any abyss will do,
deep in the Unknown to find the new!
Charles-Pierre Baudelaire
—J.H.

TO MY DAUGHTER, ZOE,
AND MY MOTHER, ANN,
for all the songs we've shared,
for all the seasons to come.
—S.S.

The Sun sings gold in the pale sky of morning,
echoing across the summer hills.
His voice grows stronger as he rises,
spilling cascades of fire along the edges of the world.

Summer's song.
Hear the summer's sunshine song.

The grass in the meadow clicks and clatters
in the fierce heat
as grasshoppers leap into their jagged flight
through the hot, humming air.
The wide river retreats into the dry earth,
becoming a sleepy flow.

The Sun sleeps
in the long star-filled evening.
Foxes creep along the river's naked banks,
leaving their cautious footsteps
in the red clay of the river's long memory.

Summer's song.
Listen to summer's golden song.

Now the summer days begin to fade.
The long and lingering evenings of August
diminish hour by hour.
The great Sun deserts the sky,
leaving an early darkness
where there had been a long, lean light.
Trees tremble in a northern breeze,
wrapped in leaves so hungry for the Sun
they carry tracings of his red and yellow light.

Autumn's song.
Hear the autumn's melancholy song.

The last unfurling flowers linger
amid an endless tide of grass.
Suddenly a great wind
thrusts itself against the trees
and billows upward in a storm of leaves.

Now the days are deserted by the birds
that stream headlong and high
across the chilling sky.

Crying out against the wind,
they slip behind the white horizon
and leave the branches bare
and silent.

Autumn's song.
Listen to autumn's tuneless song.

The Moon sings silver in the blue-black sky,
echoing across the frozen lake.
Her voice grows stronger as she rises,
filling the dank night with her light,
spilling streams of mist along the edges of the world.

Winter's song.
Hear the winter's frosty song.

White rabbits leap.
Tall pines defy the cold
with their undying green.
Hawks glide in the cloudless sky,
searching for their dinner
as wary mice vanish into the frozen earth.

Whirlwinds drape the trees in crystal
and smother the fields in wide drifts of snow.
Silence descends upon every hill and hollow
but for the long, lone howling of the wind.

Winter's song.
Listen to winter's windswept song.

The frozen silence ends
as the river roars,
bursting from its icy tomb,
washing winter from its shores.
The Sun puts on his golden garments
and strides into the sky.
And now the white world resounds
with the chatter of six million droplets
endlessly falling from the trees.

The first brave buds
push through the melting snow
and fill the air with their tender scent.

Spring's song.
Listen to spring's fragrant song.

Tall trees that seemed forever lost—
fragile victims of winter's kill—
amaze the morning with their mysteries
as a new spring is born of an old winter
and life returns to the forsaken fields.
The new Sun sings his glistening song,
lighting the fragile world,
and death itself lies dead.

Nature's song.
Hear Nature's everlasting song!

A NOTE TO READERS

The bird of prey that appears throughout this book is a red-tailed hawk *(Buteo jamaicensis)*. The most common hawk in North America, red-tails have been found everywhere from the Caribbean to Canada. These hardy birds adapt to any habitat from forests to deserts, but are most often spotted soaring above wood lots and meadowlands. They nest high in trees or on cliffs and hunt animals such as mice, rabbits, and small birds. Red-tails are not at all picky about their food. They will eat anything they can catch, including earthworms, snakes, and frogs if nothing more appetizing presents itself.

Like many other hawk species, red-tails usually mate for life. In the spring, the females lay two to three eggs. Chicks are ready to leave the nest about five weeks after they hatch and reach maturity in a year. Red-tails are large hawks, averaging two feet long with a four-foot wing span, and vary widely in coloration from solid black to albino. Most adults are brown on top and white underneath, with black or brown wing tips and belly band. The most distinctive feature of this beautiful bird is the brick-red tail feathers that give it its name.